Bilingual Edition
Clean and Healthy / Limpieza y salud
Edición Bilingüe

Taking Care of My Hair
El cuidado de tu cabello

Elizabeth Vogel
Traducción al español:
Tomás González

The Rosen Publishing Group's
PowerKids Press™ & **Editorial Buenas Letras**™
New York

1

Published in 2001, 2004 by The Rosen Publishing Group, Inc.
29 East 21st Street, New York, NY 10010

Copyright © 2001, 2004 by The Rosen Publishing Group, Inc.

First Bilungual Edition 2004
First Edition in English 2001

Book Design: Danielle Primiceri
Layout: Dean Galiano

Photo Illustrations by Thaddeus Harden

Vogel, Elizabeth.
   Taking Care of My Hair = El cuidado de tu cabello / by Elizabeth Vogel ; traducción al español Tomás González
      p. cm. — (PowerKids Readers. Clean & Healthy All Day Long = Limpieza y salud todo el día)
   Includes index.
   Summary: Describes how to take care of one's hair so that it will be healthy.
   ISBN: 0-8239-6611-9 (lib. bdg. : alk. paper)
      1. Hair—Care and hygiene—Juvenile literature. [1. Hair—Care and hygiene.
   2. Spanish language materials—Bilingual]
      I. Title. II. Series.
      646.7'24—dc21

Manufactured in the United States of America

2

Contents

Contenido

Hair needs a lot of care.
I brush my hair to keep it
soft and healthy.

———————

El cabello necesita
mucho cuidado.
Debemos cepillarlo
para mantenerlo suave
y saludable.

5

I have long hair. Hair can be long or short, straight or curly.

Tengo pelo largo. El pelo puede ser corto o largo, lacio o rizado.

Sometimes I wear barrettes in my hair. Barrettes keep my hair neat.

A veces llevo broches para el pelo. Los broches, o hebillas, mantienen ordenado el cabello.

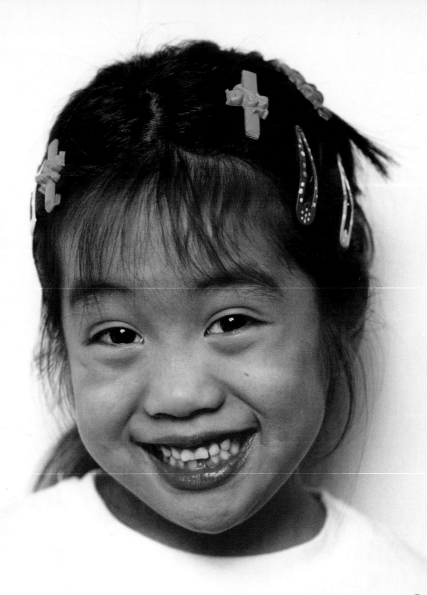

Sometimes I wear my hair down. It is fun to wear my hair different ways.

A veces me dejo el pelo suelto. Es divertido llevar el pelo de distintas formas.

Healthy hair grows six inches each year. I go to the hairdresser to get my hair cut. Haircuts keep my hair healthy.

El pelo saludable crece seis pulgadas cada año. Voy a la peluquería para que me lo corten. Así se mantiene sano.

13

Every type of hair needs to be cut. The hairdresser uses scissors to cut my hair.

Todos los tipos de cabello necesitan cortarse. La peluquera usa tijeras para cortarme el pelo.

14

First the hairdresser washes my hair. She uses shampoo. Shampoo washes the dirt out of my hair.

Primero, la peluquera me lava el pelo con champú. El champú limpia la mugre de mi cabello.

16

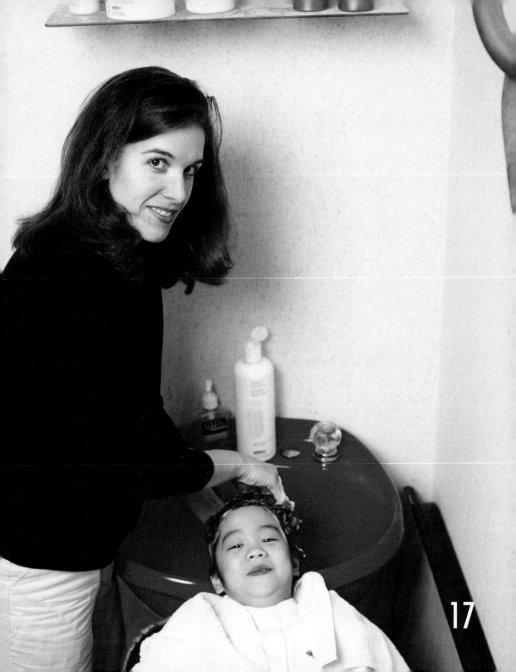

17

Then the hairdresser rinses
the shampoo out of my
hair. She makes sure all
the soapy bubbles
are gone.

Después, la peluquera
me enjuaga el champú y
se asegura de que no
quede nada de espuma.

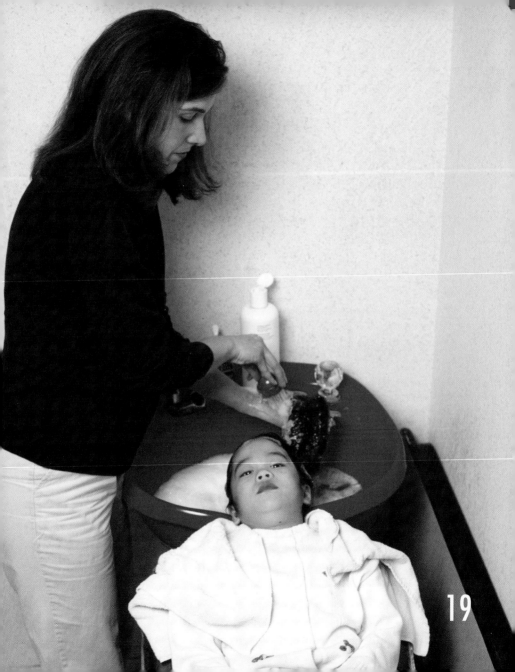

19

I wash my hair at home, too. I use a comb when my hair is wet. Combing my hair helps to keep tangles out. I love to take care of my clean and healthy hair!

También en mi casa me lavo el cabello. Lo peino con un peine mientras está mojado. Al peinar el pelo evito que se enrede. ¡Me encanta cuidar de mi cabello limpio y saludable!

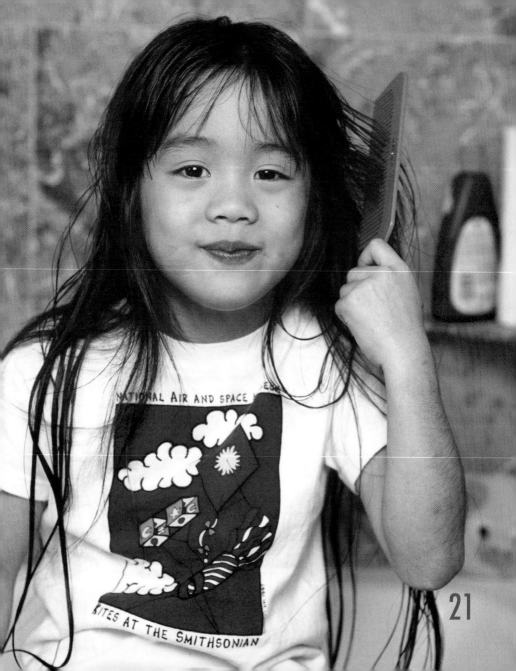

21

Words to Know
Palabras que debes saber

BARRETTES /
BROCHES O HEBILLAS

BRUSH /
CEPILLO

COMB /
PEINE

HAIRDRESSER /
PELUQUERA

SHAMPOO /
CHAMPÚ

Here are more books to read about taking care of your hair / Otros libros que puedes leer sobre el cuidado del cabello:

In English / En inglés:
My Hair is Beautiful: Because It is Mine
Por Paula Dejoie
Writers & Readers Publishing, Inc.

Bilingual Editions / Ediciones bilingües:
Hair/Pelo (Lets Read About our Bodies)
Por Cynthia Klingel
Gareth Stevens, January 2002

Due to the changing nature of Internet links, PowerKids Press has developed an online list of Web sites related to the subject of this book. This site is updated regularly. Please use this link to access the list:

http://www.buenasletraslinks.com/chl/tch

Index

Índice

Words in English: 165   Palabras en español: 162

Note to Parents, Teachers, and Librarians

PowerKids Readers en Español are specially designed to get emergent and beginning hispanic readers excited about learning to read. Simple stories and concepts are paired with photographs of real kids in real-life situations. Sentences are short and simple, employing a basic vocabulary of sight words, as well as new words that describe familiar things and places. With their engaging stories and vivid photo-illustrations, PowerKids en Español gives children the opportunity to develop a love of reading and learning that they will carry with them throughout their lives.